Moonlight of Morgan Hill

Patricia Tracy Dow Beveridge

XULON PRESS

Xulon Press
2301 Lucien Way #415
Maitland, FL 32751
407.339.4217
www.xulonpress.com

© 2017 by Patricia Tracy Dow Beveridge

Cover and Interior design by Cecille Kaye Gumadan

Illustrations by Patricia Dow Beveridge

All rights reserved solely by the author. The author guarantees all contents are original and do not infringe upon the legal rights of any other person or work. No part of this book may be reproduced in any form without the permission of the author. The views expressed in this book are not necessarily those of the publisher.

Printed in the United States of America.

ISBN-13: 9781545609804

Moonlight of Morgan Hill

Patricia Tracy Dow Beveridge

Dedication

For my dear grandchildren, Gusty whose exuberance for sports is awesome and for Callen, builder extraordinaire of Legos and lover of John Denver's "Country Road."

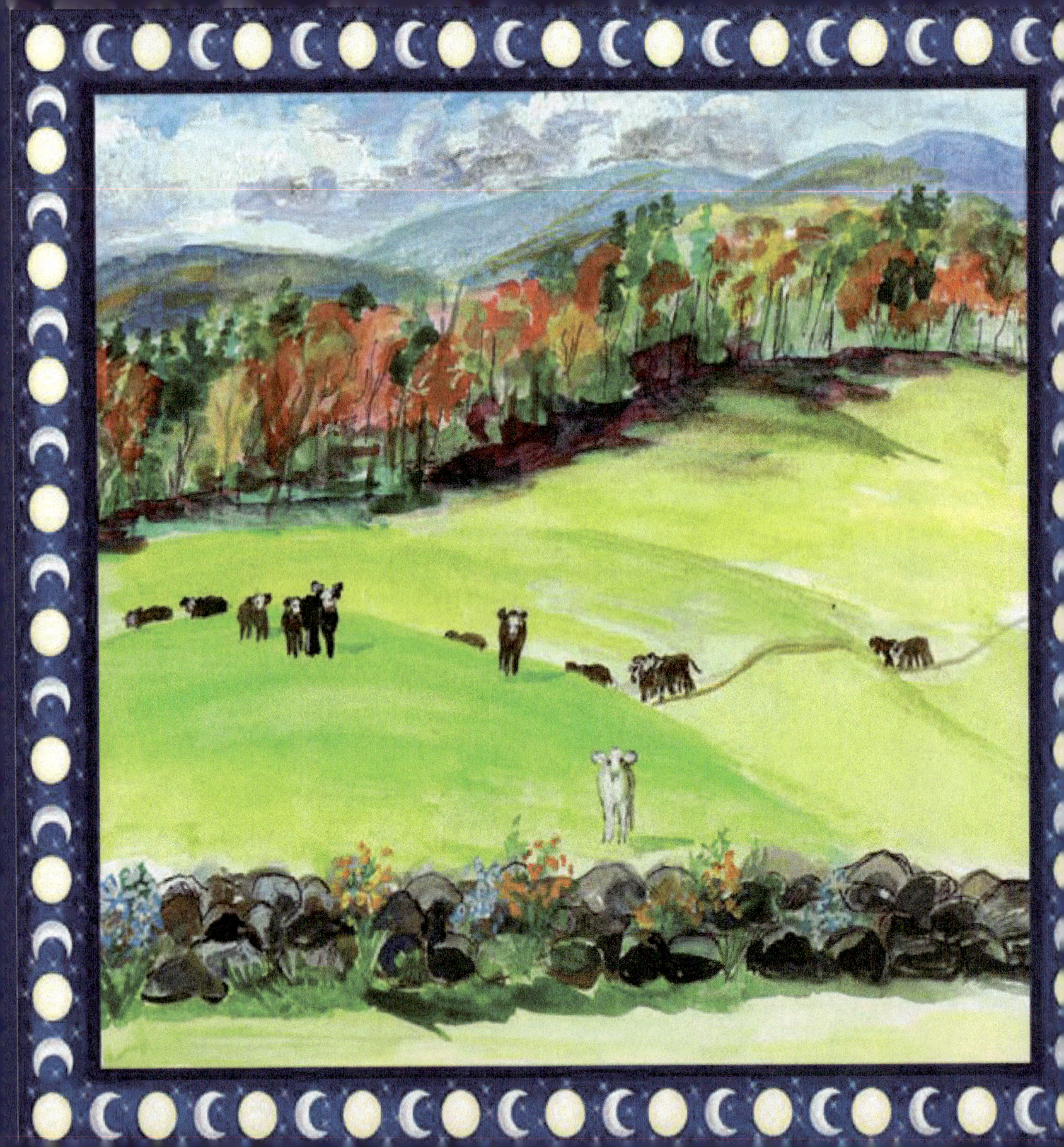

She was a beautiful cow, the color of the moon, grazing on a hillside in Vermont. And one fall, I painted her. The leaves were at their peak. The days were warm. It was the ideal time to paint. The reds were progressing over the hills with each passing day, and yet the shades of green were still vibrant. It was my favorite time to paint because Indian summer can pass very quickly. The leaves are soon on the ground if the rains are heavy and the wind strong. Every day, as I set up my easel, the cows would come out of the valley, up the hill, as if on cue, to stand at the fence and watch me paint.

There she was. She would stand right at the fence exactly where she should to enhance my composition. For the first fifteen minutes, she would look at me and stand perfectly still, beckoning me to paint her. The others would stand momentarily and move away, but she stood and looked directly at me. I never planned to have cows in this particular painting although they have been the subjects of much of my work. However, I decided to include her in the painting. She was the color of moonlight, and I really wanted a rich brown cow in that corner of the painting to help the composition, so I painted her body in a rich burnt sienna and her lovely face white. I had no idea how special she was until I learned her story...

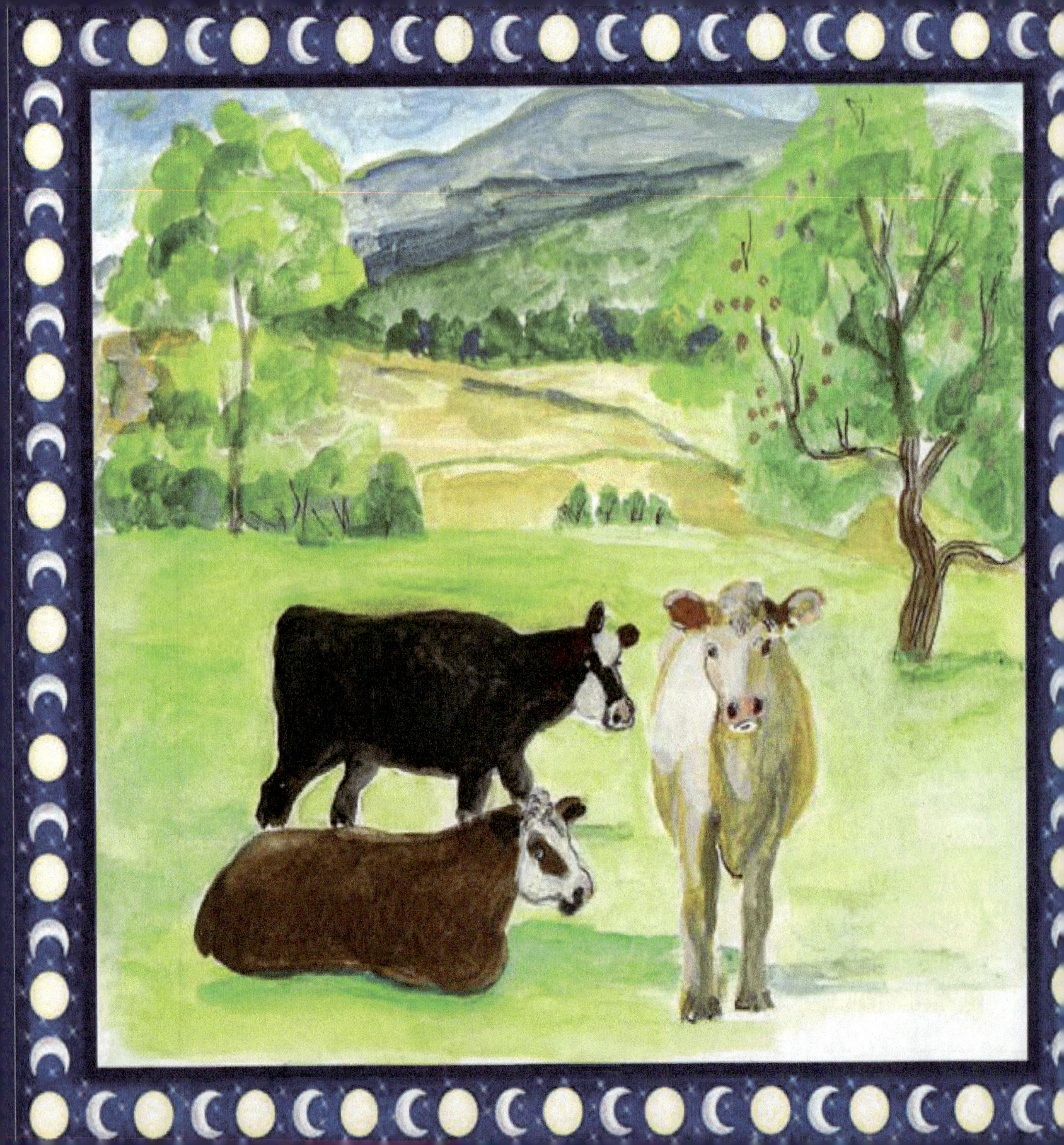

Moonlight was born in Vermont at a place called Morgan Hill Farm. The marker on the hill reads, "In 1777, Jacob Morgan camped on Morgan Hill on his way to the Battle of Bennington."* Charmed by its beauty, he returned after the war and built his home there and gave Morgan Hill its name.

Some 236 years later, Moonlight lived on Morgan Hill with a small herd of mostly Hereford cows. She and her mother cow friends produced the babies that arrived every spring. Her best friends were Patches and Bandit. They were older cows and had seen many young cows, but they had never known one quite like Moonlight. They were very fond of her.

---

*The Battle of Bennington was an important battle of the American revolutionary war, fought on August 16, 1777 in a field in Hoosick, New York, near the town of Bennington, Vermont.

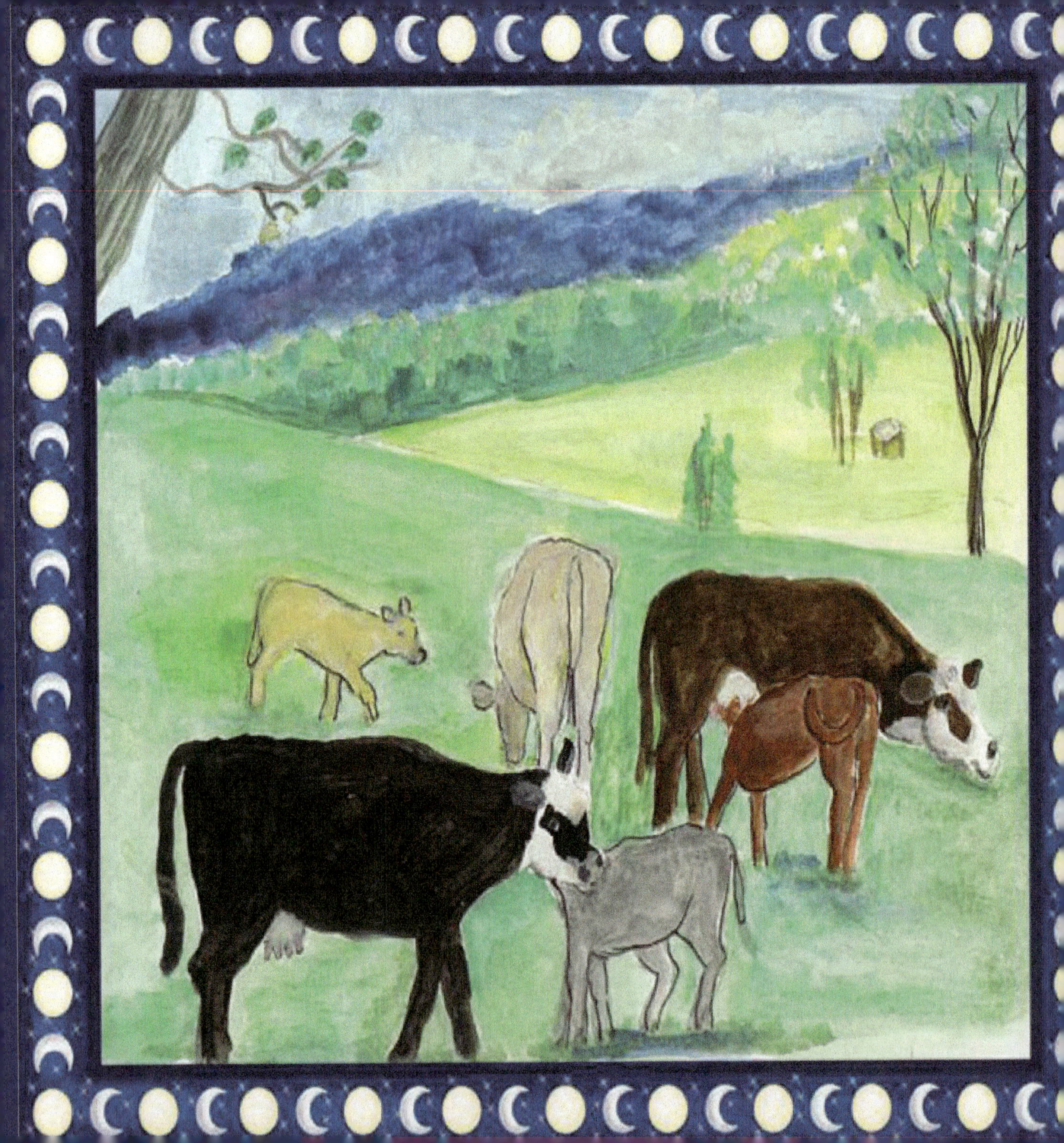

In late summer, Patches, Bandit, and Moonlight all had their babies at about the same time. Patches and Bandit's babies were gray and brown; Moonlight's baby had a light coat like his mom, but it had flecks of gold in it. She decided to call him Nugget.

Moonlight was always happy and full of fun. Many times she heard the farmhand's remark on how beautiful she was, and she was very proud of herself and Nugget. In fact, when the artist came to paint that fall, she would always be the first one up the hill to pose for her. She stood very still so the artist could paint her and fully appreciate her beauty and her gorgeous, luminous coat. She told Patches and Bandit that she would be famous, and everyone would remember her as the most beautiful cow in Vermont.

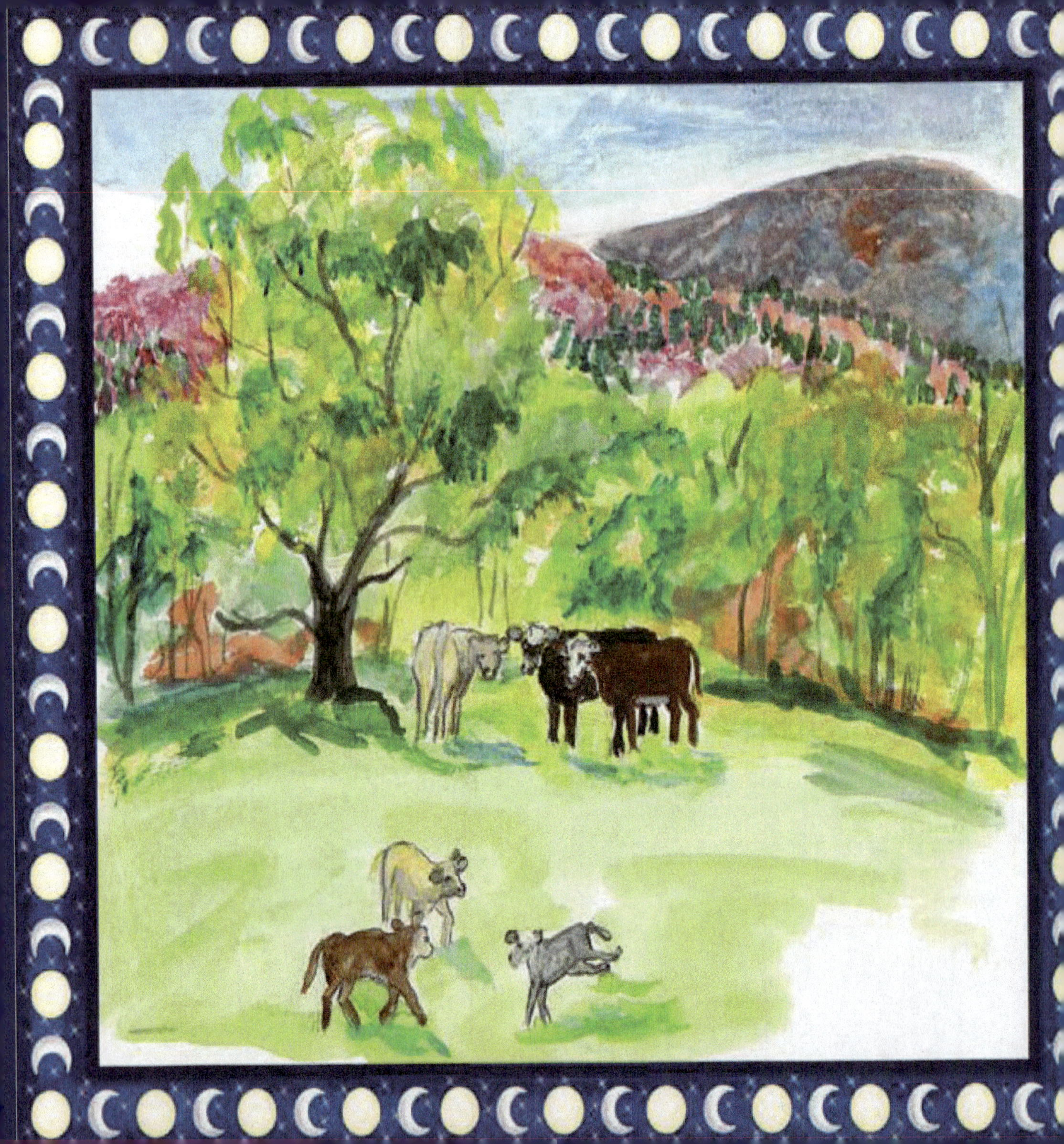

One day as Patches and Bandit were standing under an old maple tree splendid in the golden colors of autumn, softly chewing the luscious green grass of September and watching their babies frolic, Moonlight told them how the artist had looked and looked at her, and she knew it was because she was so beautiful, and that she would soon be famous.

"You know there are much more important reasons to be remembered than how you look, Moonlight," said Patches. "It really is what is in your heart that is important."

Moonlight wasn't convinced. She said that just the other day the owner had remarked to another man how beautiful she was and how he hoped she would have more calves that had her beautiful moonlight-colored coat.

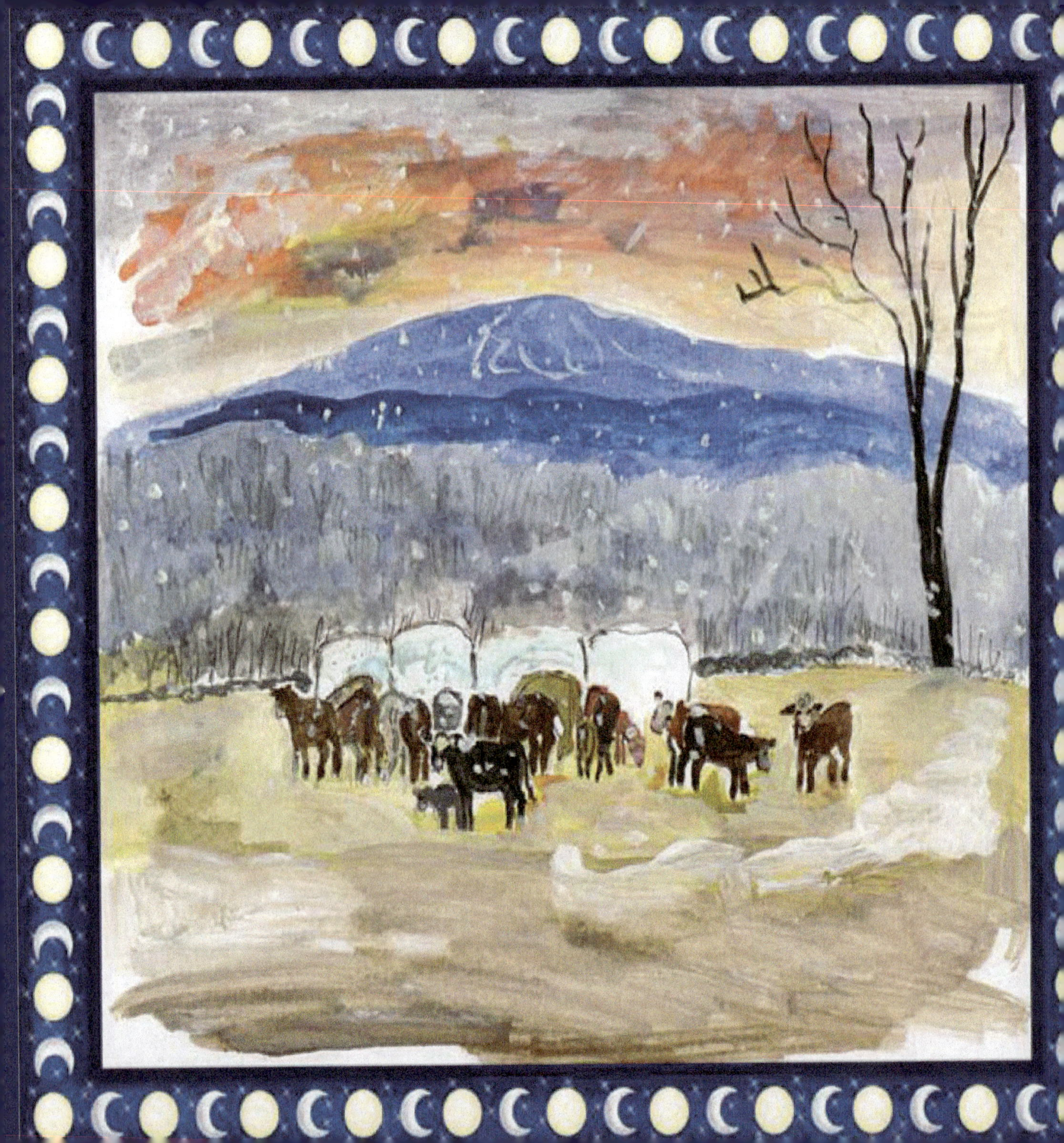

As late fall came upon the hillsides, the days became shorter and the cold winds started to blow. All the cows began to grow their coarse winter fur. Moonlight was not happy. She didn't like her winter coat because it wasn't as beautiful as her silky summer one. It was dull and not the color of the moon.

As fall lapsed into winter, the herd huddled together for warmth and since Patches, Bandit, and Moonlight had the youngest babies (most of the others were born in the spring), they stood in the center of the herd where they would be the warmest. The nights came early, the snow started to fly, and it was very cold.

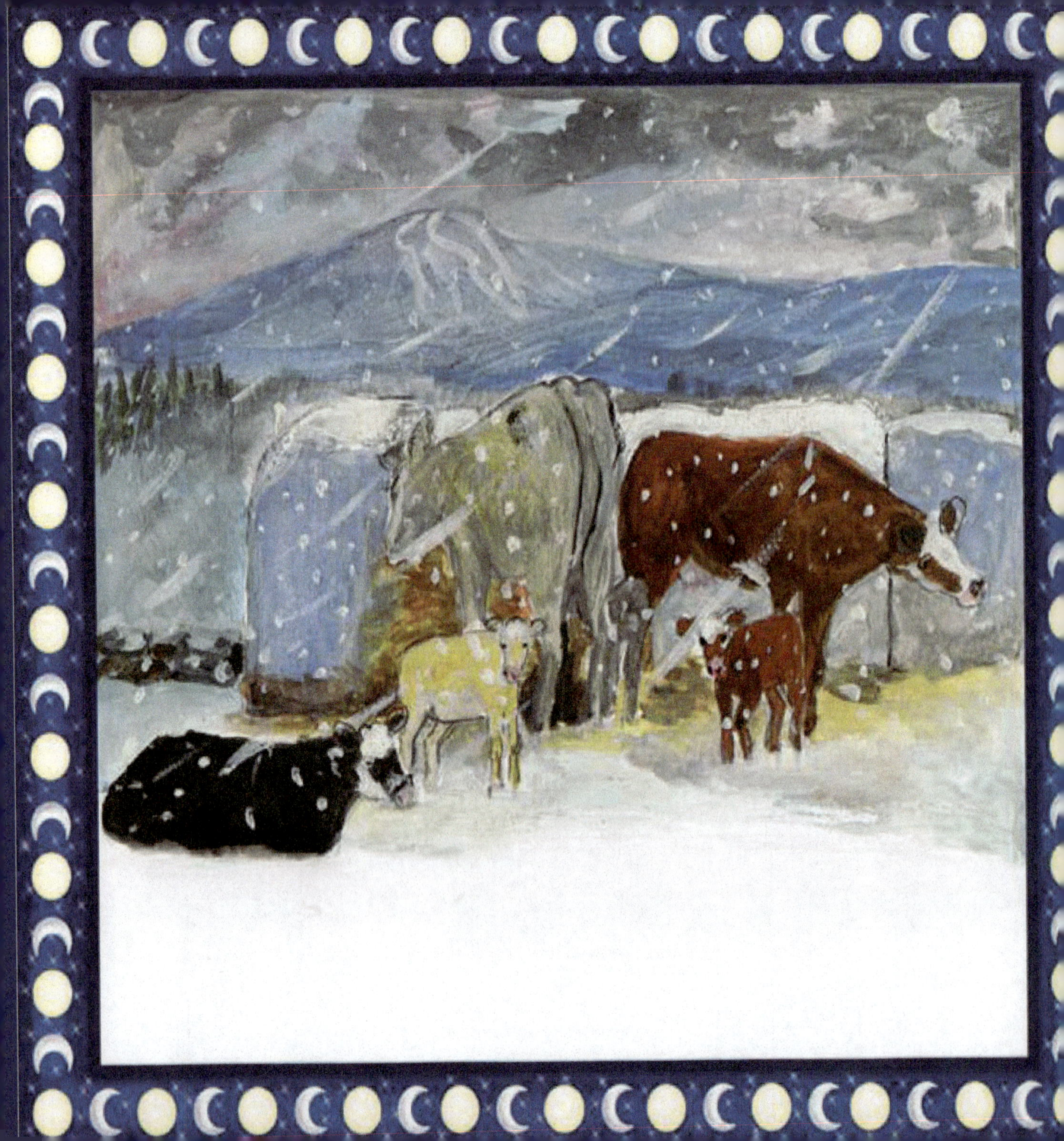

One day, Patches and Bandit started to feel poorly. Tired with the cold and feeling ill, they were unable to nurse their babies. Moonlight was very concerned. She said, "Don't worry, I'll feed the babies." Patches thought she would not have enough. However, Moonlight was not frightened. She said she would have enough and that enough is a lot. "Let the babies all take turns, and you and Bandit rest," she said.

Through the frigid days of January and February, she stood by the hay bale, nursing all three babies. She kept eating the hay and feeding the babies day and night as the winter winds blew. She became thinner by the day, but the milk still flowed.

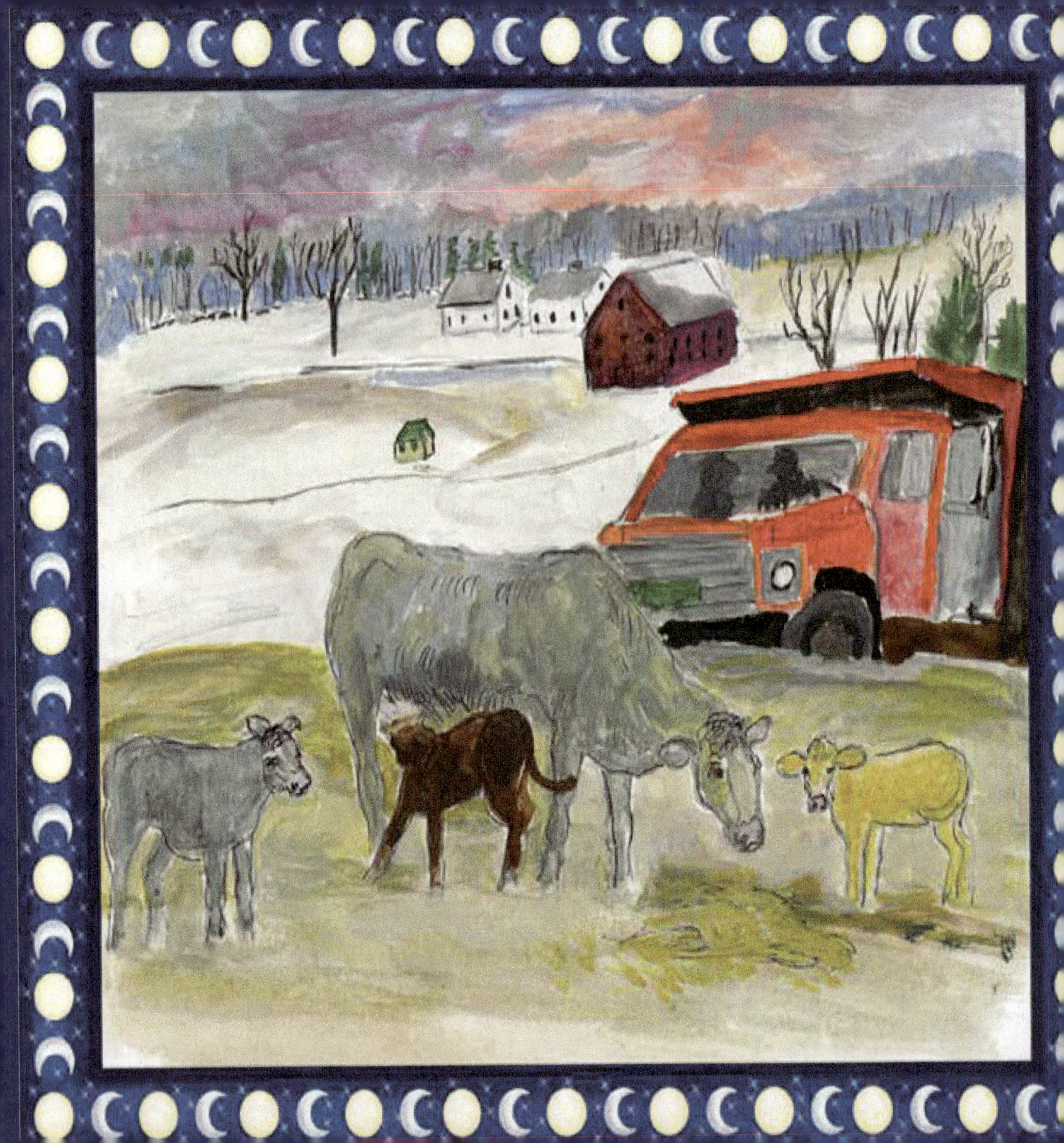

Soon Patches and Bandit did start to feel better, but their milk was still too little. Without complaint, Moonlight continued to feed the babies. By then it was February, and there was a stretch to the evening light. Soon the farmers would be gathering the sap for the maple syrup as the days became warmer. Because of her heavy winter coat, they didn't notice how thin Moonlight had become. However, they did notice how fat the three late summer babies were, and they were very pleased.

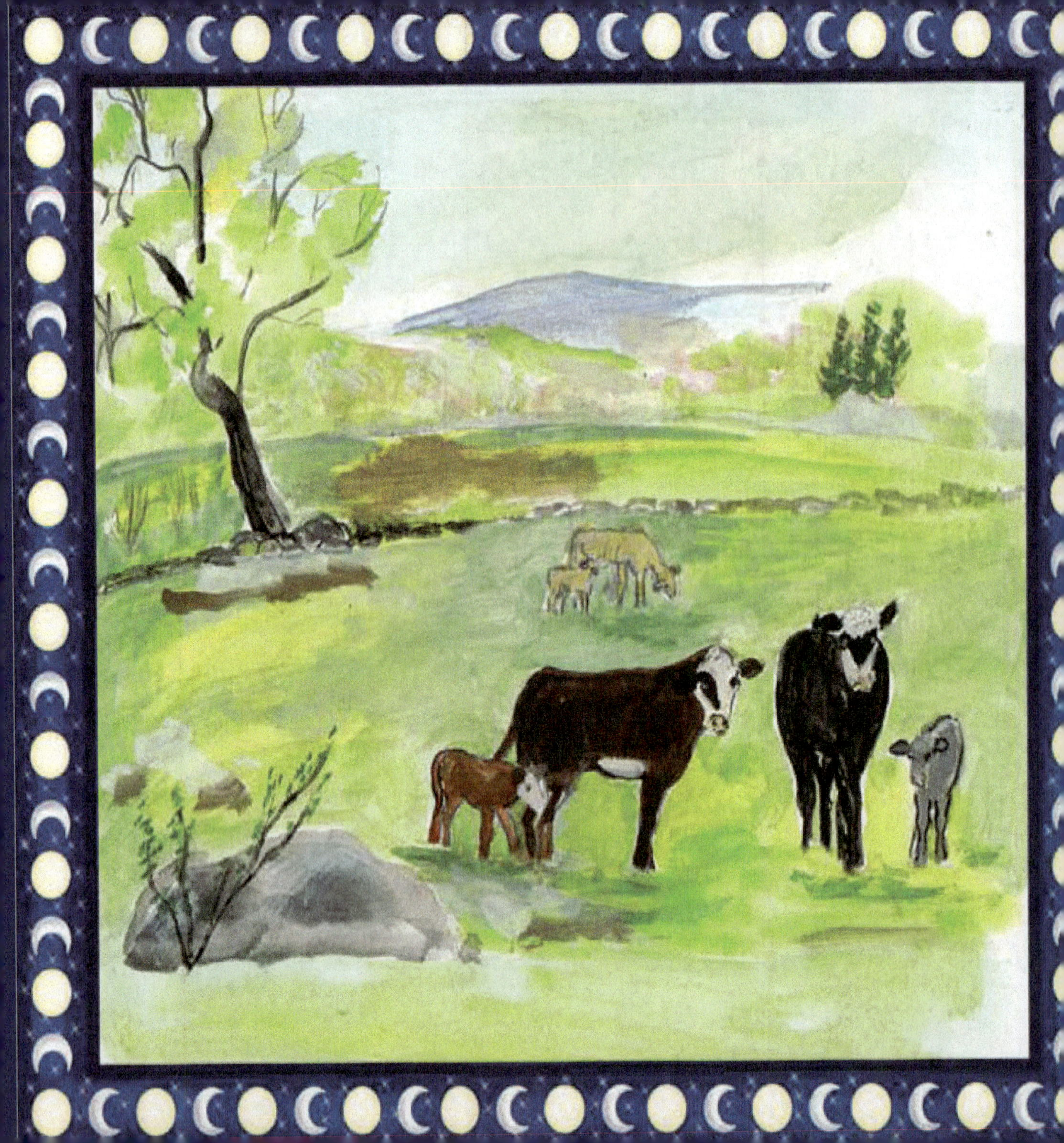

As spring arrived, Patches and Bandit began to feed their babies again, and the winter snow started to recede. They were so grateful that Moonlight had taken such good care of the babies. She never once complained, and Nugget never once was jealous of the other babies drinking his mom's milk. Moonlight had raised him well.

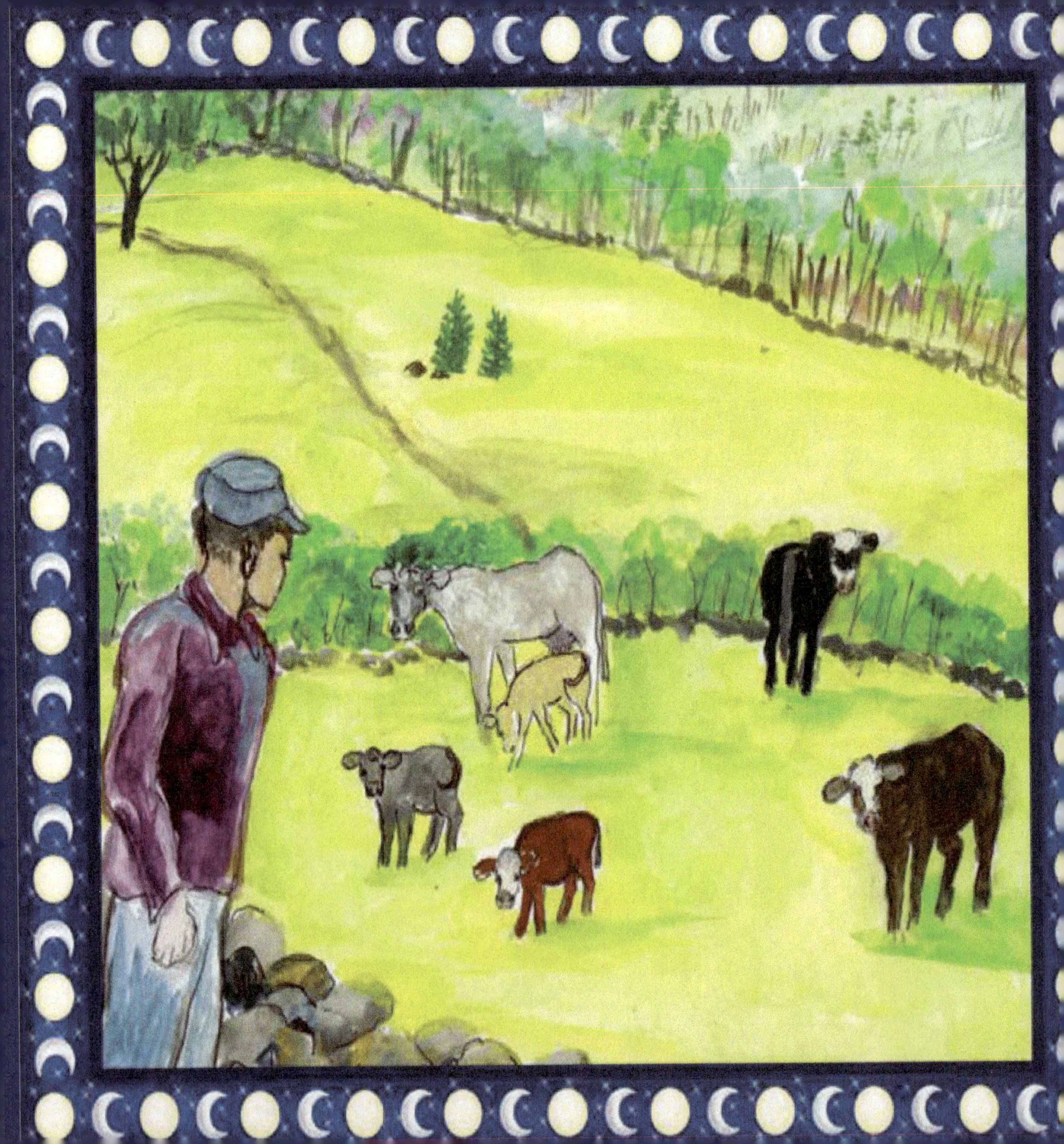

When the farmer came to check the herd, he noticed how thin Moonlight had become. He was quite worried about the beautiful young cow that now had a dull coat and had become so thin. She definitely was not the color of moonlight. Next to her stood her beautiful son and the two fat babies of Patches and Bandit.

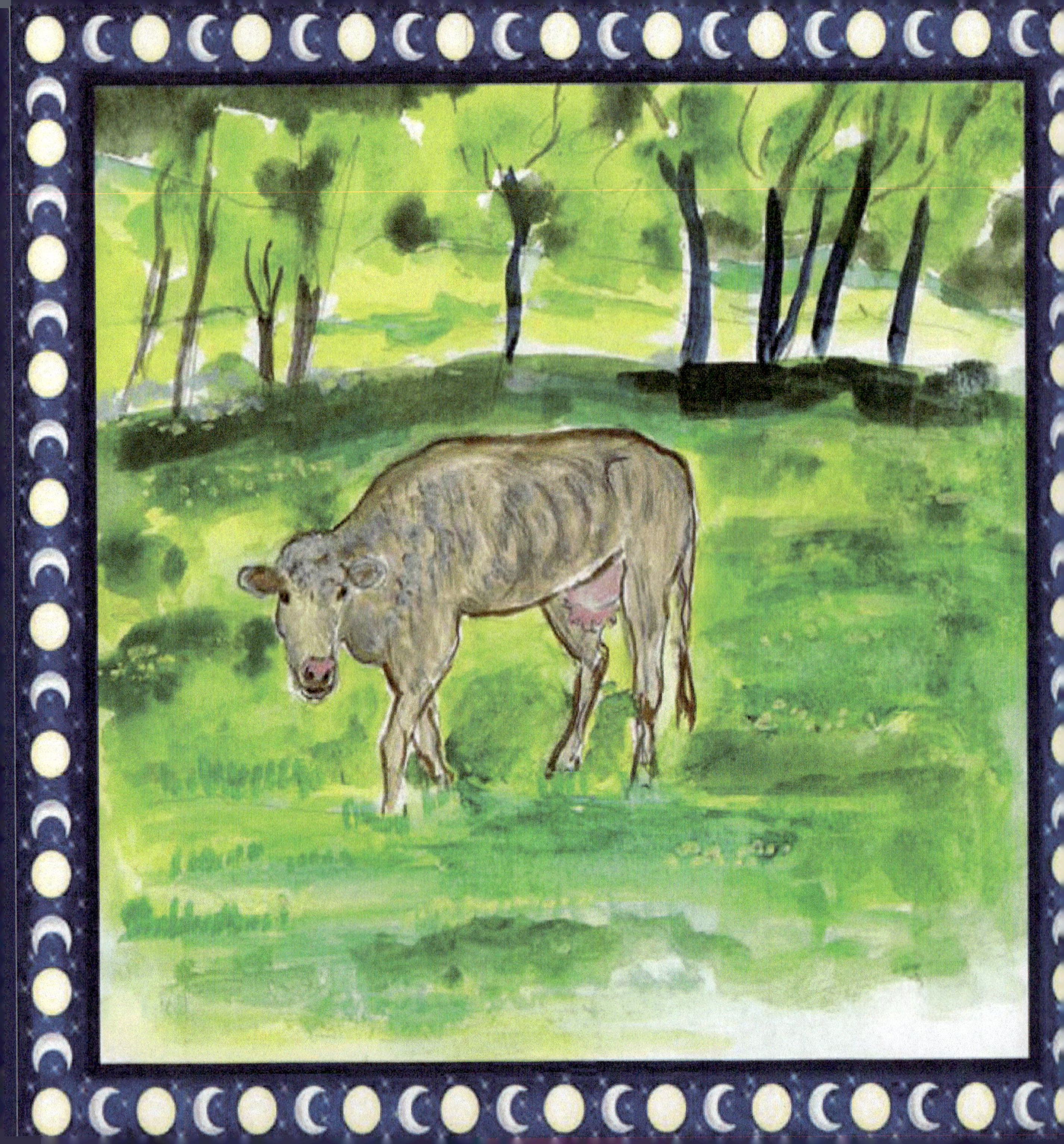

The cows told Moonlight every day how much they admired her. But Moonlight wasn't listening. She turned inward and stood listlessly in the meadow. She was very sad that she had lost her beautiful coat. She was sure it would never return. She missed the compliments of the farmhand and the farmer. She was very discouraged about her situation. Her perception about herself was wrong. Now *perception* is a big word, and it means, her thought about herself. She thought that because she was not pretty anymore, she was not worthwhile. Even though her friends told her that what she did for the calves, through her courage and generosity, was wonderful, she didn't believe them. You see, what you think of yourself is very important to your well-being.

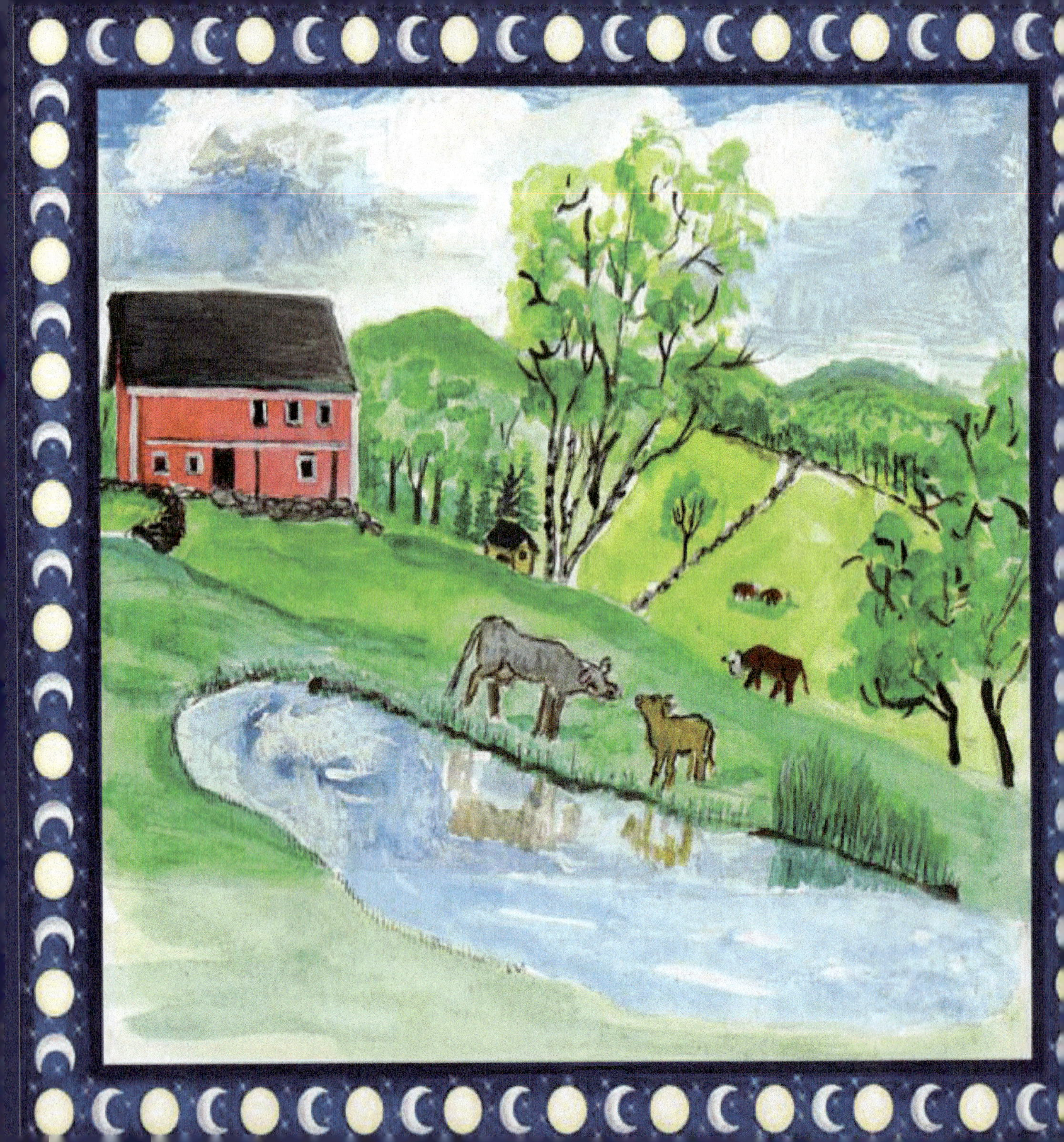

One day, Nugget asked Moonlight, "Who is God?"

Well, Moonlight had never thought much about God. She asked how he had heard about God. He told her that Patches and Bandit talked about God a lot. "And what did they say about God?" she asked.

"They said God was in our soul, and if we listen to God, we will always do the right thing. That is how we reflect God."

Now *reflect* is an interesting word too. When we look in a mirror, our face is reflected back to us. If we do the right thing, God is reflected in us.

Nugget told her that Bandit said to him that his mom reflected God. "She said it was because you generously fed us all winter long and never thought about yourself. They said you have a beautiful soul."

Moonlight stopped chewing for a moment to reflect on what Nugget had said. Now the word *reflect* also has another meaning. It means to think about something, or to reflect on it. She liked the idea of God and her soul being beautiful. She had never thought that way before. Nugget had given Moonlight something to think about.

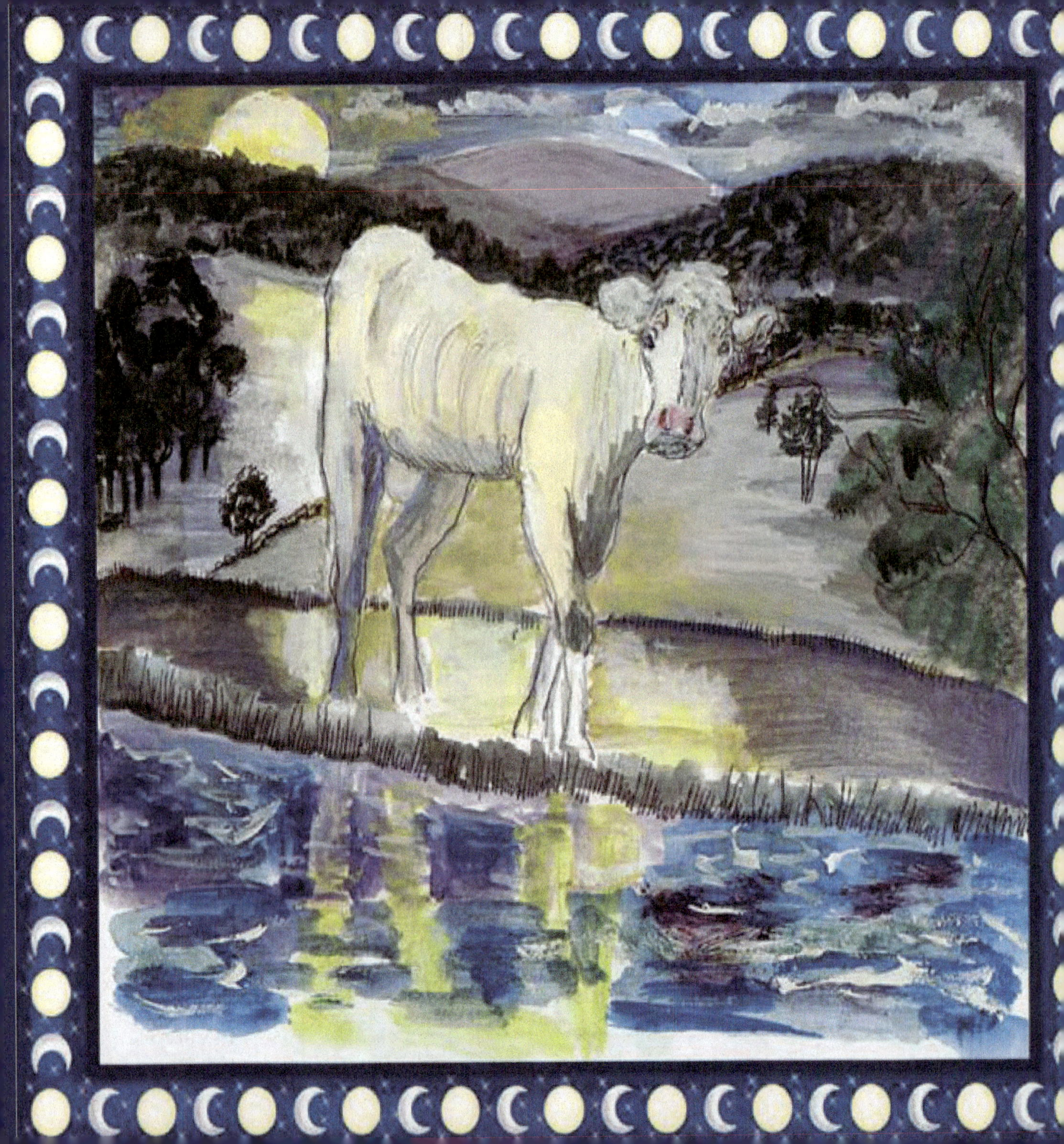

Slowly, Moonlight began to feel better about herself. She felt change coming over her. Yes, her perception of herself began to change. She began to think that by reflecting God, she became beautiful in her soul. Even if she was no longer beautiful on the outside, she knew that when she reflected God, she was beautiful on the inside. She began to see that it was love for Bandit and Patches, their babies, and Nugget that had caused her to do what she did. She was reflecting God's love much like the moon reflects the light of the sun.

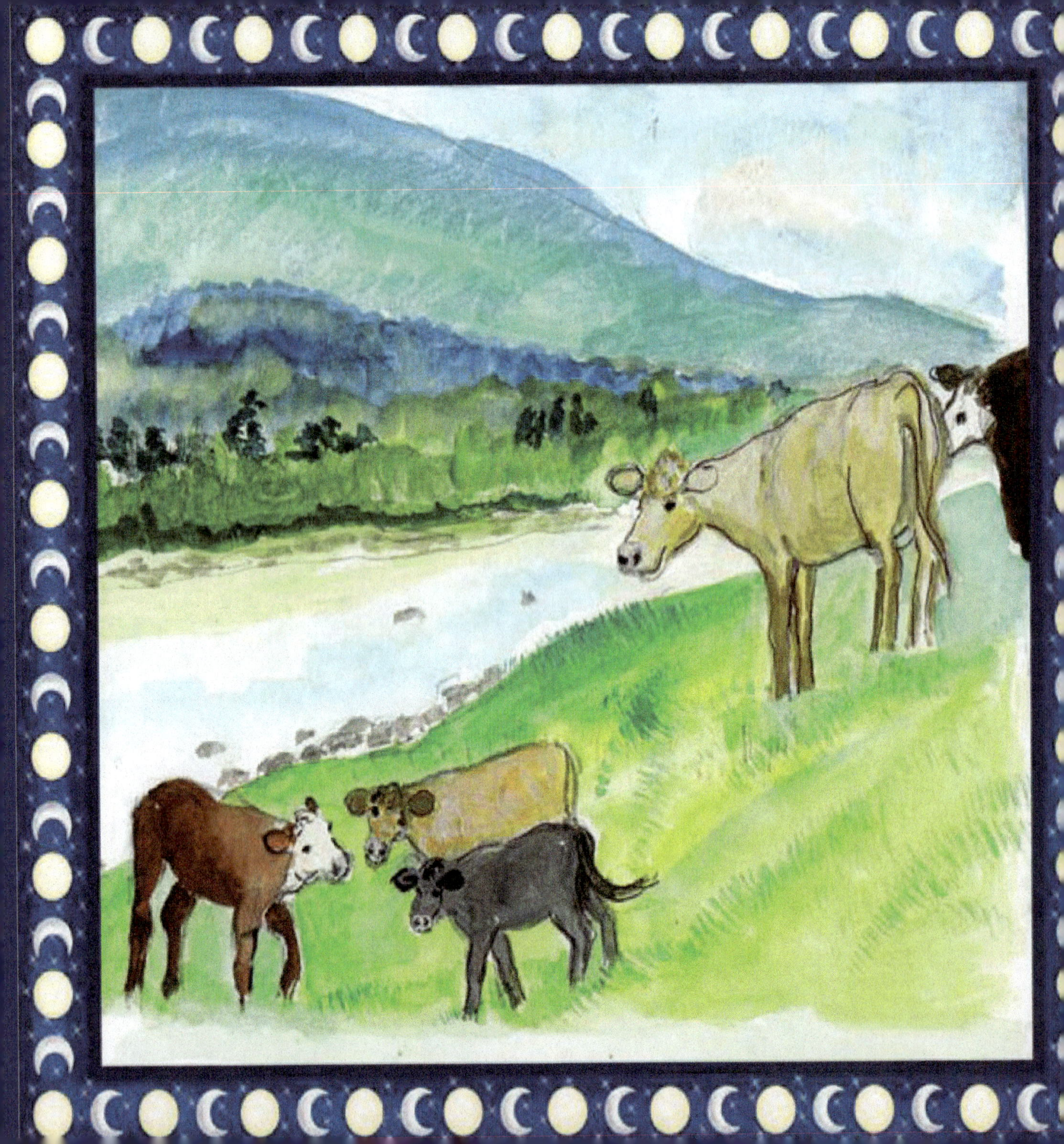

For the first time in months, she lifted her head and smelled the spring breezes. She noticed the leaves unfurling on the trees. She watched the young calves frolicking in the meadow. She wasn't looking inward anymore. She felt a smile coming from deep inside of her. She went back into the herd. She wanted to know all about how the cows were doing. She began to participate in the planning of which part of the pasture they would be grazing in each day. She became herself again, the happy young cow that she was before. Do you know what else? Her coat began to shine more beautifully than ever. In fact, it glowed!

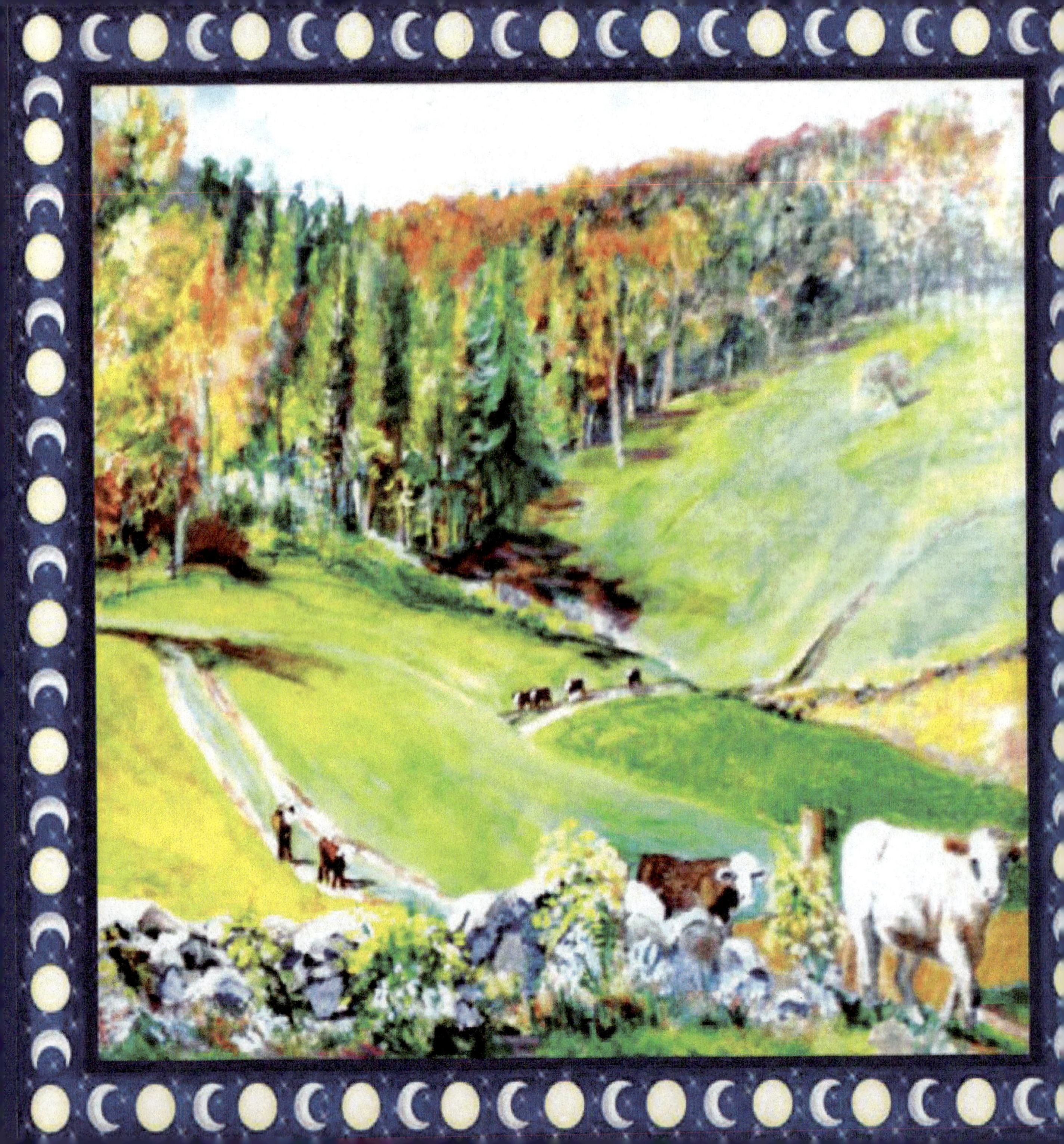

That fall I saw her again. Because the wise old owl that keeps watch over Morgan Hill had told me what she had done, I painted her again. This time I painted her the glorious color of moonlight. I was honored to paint the gorgeous cow with the sunlight in her beautiful soul.

Acknowledgements

Special thanks to Kerri at the Wilder Memorial Library for her help in steering me through the intricacies of the computers, as well as to Bob and Linda for my night visits to their computer at the Inn, to my English-teacher daughter Christie for her help in editing, to Peter Sharp who lets me wander through his fields in search of the perfect painting, and to Dave and Dimity who brought me to Morgan Hill in the first place.

CPSIA information can be obtained
at www.ICGtesting.com
Printed in the USA
BVOW07s2349081017
496654BV00001BA/1/P

9 781545 609804